Introduction

After the success of "**Thrumming Heart**" becoming a bestseller on Amazon 2022 and receiving a bronze medal "short stories" genre in the C I am writing this book, Ticl funny English stories so, wh have received some bad new bright up your day. I want to is the best cure.

I want to thank Hannah Curtis and Andrew Thornton for creating the book cover, and Chaye'lee Mcquade and Marisa Straccia and her team for helping me for the forthcoming graphic novel, turning each story of "Thrumming Heart" into graphics. When I go to Comic-con, I find that people like different methods for enjoying books: audiobook, graphic novels and paperbacks and e-books so I have published "Thrumming Heart" in all the formats.

In this book, you will find part of the writing in bold italic; these parts represent the character's thoughts.

After reading this book, please visit Amazon.co.uk or Amazon.com and write a review.

Please go to the following link for competitions, book releases, and latest updates of Paolo Debernardi's TV, film, and theatre appearances:

https://form.aweber.com/form/11/351188711.htm

The Author
Paolo Debernardi

TICKLE HEART

VOLUME 1

A COLLECTION OF FUNNY SHORT STORIES

Paolo Debernardi

ISBN 978-1-916838-61-1 (Pbk)
ISBN 978-1-916838-62-8 (e-book)

Printed by Biddles Books Limited,
King's Lynn, Norfolk

Contents

The freaky clown

Knock, knock.

"Who is it?"

"It's me, Lillian. Open the door."

"Who's whom?"

"It's me, Lilian. Open the door," an enraged voice repeats.

Lillian peers from the bottom window of the living room. She jumps a little and covers her mouth with her right hand in terror.

"What's wrong, Lilly? Right now, I'm preparing dinner. I don't have a minute to spare. I wish your dad was here helping me out."

"There is man standing outside and his name is 'it's me'," pointing with her index finger.

The stranger waves and smiles. The two canine teeth, like vampire teeth, appear and overlap his bottom lip.

"Can you describe him?"

"He is wearing long, brown, clown shoes, harlequin top and trousers. He has an enormous red nose, ruby, chubby lips, white circles covering his eyes and black afro hair. He is holding hostage our beloved dog, Jesse."

"That description sounds to me like your dafty father – let him in."

"Mom, mom, clowns freak me out."

"Lillian, go to your room and play; I'll deal with him."

Mollie storms in the living room; before opening the door, she dries up her hands on the *Rambo First Blood* apron.

The front door opens wide.

"You've done it again!"

"I've done what?" Ben grills.

"You've freaked out Lillian with your clown costume."

"You know that tomorrow I am in a play in her school. I'm perfecting my acting."

"Now you can perfect your cooking skills!"

Ben walks inside and, with every step, his shoes squeak on the carpet.

In Lillian's bedroom, she hears the heated quarrel escalating to swooshing, flying, porcelain plates, which shatter on the kitchen laminate floor.

"Oh no, again!" Lillian shouts, slapping her face and shaking her head.

Secret confession

In the McDonald car park, inside a blue DS3, Jessica was sobbing. Her tears were rolling down her pink cheeks. Her phone whistled. Another Facebook message came through. "Hi Jessica, are you free this evening?"

Ping! Her phone received a text message. "Jessica, it had been a while since we went out. How are you?"

Whistle, ping, whistle, ping, whistle, ping.

"No, again! Why can't they give me peace?"

"Are you okay, Jessica?", Jeremy rubbed her shoulder in attempt to comfort her.

"If I knew, I would have brought my scuba-diving gear. I'm drowning here."

"All these boys and older men, don't leave me alone. They text and Facebook message me all the time."

"I can imagine. You are so stunning."

"Thanks"

"No man can resist you. Your long, blonde hair and your flirtatious, puppy eyes are like love spells."

"Tell me about it."

"I might have a solution."

"Please, Jeremy." Jessica stared at him with big, puppy eyes.

"You can't say you're a lesbian. You don't want to do that. You become even more hot, irresistible to men. We don't want that, do we?"

"Certainly, not!"

Jeremy scratched his head. An idea popped in his mind. "I think I got it."

"I always believe in you. You always come up with solutions for problems, Jeremy."

"Thanks Jessica, next time you find yourself in a sticky, sensual situation, say, in a deep voice, 'I used to be a man'."

Jessica stopped sobbing and burst out laughing.

"You always know what to say to make me feel good."

"I'm glad I can help you."

Next day, in a park, Jessica had arranged a meeting with Andrew.

"Last night, Jessica phoned me saying she needs to talk. It's an important matter we need to discuss. Oh, no, she's going to end our friendship with benefits. It had been more than 10 years since I had sex with a woman before I met Jessica. My last girlfriend cheated on me with my best friend, and she dumped me on my birthday. I hope it's something else."

Andrew was walking on the path.

Jessica was sitting on the bench; as soon as she saw him, she waved.

"Howl, howl, sticking out my tongue. Oh my god, she is hotter than ever. Her black leather, high-heel shoes and her skinny dress compliment her figure."

"Hi Andrew, how are you?"

"I'm great thanks." Sipping his coffee, an attempt of sugar-coat an unexpected disappointment or bad news.

Jessica turned her head right and inhaled some gas from the balloon inside her Louis Vuitton handbag. She turned her head straight to Jeremy. With a wide, confident smile, she exclaimed "I'm used to be a man!"

"What?" Andrew coughed.

"Are you okay?"

"Yes, the coffee went down to the wrong direction."

"That's impossible! She's so perfect."

"How can it be? You're so perfect."

"Today, plastic surgent can do miracles."

"Come on, Jeremy, find an excuse."

"Oh Jessica, I need to go."

"So soon, Andrew?"

"Yes, I remember my mum has given me some chores to do. I completely forgot until now. You know mums, they are a pest. They keep reminding you until you have done what they ask."

Andrew walked away from the bench. His walk turned into a run.

"Run, run Andrew. Away from her."

"Hold a sec, Andrew; your mum died in a car accident 2 years ago."

Andrew was already too far away to hear Jessica.

In the path, Andrew had started texting to all the boys and men Jessica had dated in the past. They all coughed and found an excuse to be somewhere else.

"I'll brush my teeth, gargle with mouthwash a couple of times, have a cold shower and burn all the clothes I wore while I was dating Jessica. Purification of my mind and soul, exercise temptation."

Hidden

In a car park outside of Tesco supermarket.

"Jack, what can you see?"

"I can see Tesco supermarket."

"Great, what about much closer to you?"

"I can see a red Porsche 911 Carrera parked. It is my favourite car in the world."

"Brilliant, what about next to you?"

"I can see my dearest and lovely girlfriend, Sara, the love of my life." "I love you, darling."

"I love you too, Jack."

"Fantastic, what about in front of your eyes?"

"I can see your index finger."

"You got it, I hide very well."

Sweet craving

Inside the Tesco supermarket, mum and son went to do the main shopping.

"Mum, this week I had been a good boy. Can you buy me some ice cream?"

"Yes, you have; of course, I will".

In the distance, Mollie saw her best friend, Janet.

"Before I buy you some ice cream, can I talk to Janet?"

"Mum, you promise you buy me some ice cream."

"I will; be patient Mark."

Mollie dragged Mark and approached Janet.

"Hi Janet; how are you?"

"Great; I am a bit hung-over from going out last night."

"Of course. It's a pity I could not go out. I could not get a babysitter."

"That's a shame, John came out last night. He was asking about you."

"Mum, the ice cream."

"Wait a sec, can't you see adults are talking? What did you say?"

"I said you probably were too busy."

"What was the plan yesterday?"

"We met up in a pub and moved to the nightclub you like until the early hours of the morning. It was the best night I have had for ages."

"Mum, the ice cream. I'm dying here", pulling his mum's skirt.

"Don't think so, Mark. He is usually a good boy. Today he is having a tantrum. What a pity I could not go out; next time, I will."

"Mum, you promised you'd buy me some ice cream. Ice cream. I want ice cream," stamping on the tile floor, spinning the shopping trolley around. His hands went through the shelves, knocking down the boxes of food onto the floor.

Mollie took a deep breath, stared at Mark with a warm, broad smile.

"Darling, I'm not your mum. I don't know who your mum is."

"Mum? Mum!"

The parrot

"Don't answer the door tomorrow, for any reason."

"What if it is an emergency and the police knocks on the door?!"

"What I said, do not answer the door, mother."

"I am elderly, not daft."

"I'm sorry mum. I'm stressed out."

"I forgive you."

Next day, Queen Street was deserted; so far, no one had dared knocking number 25 Queen Street. It was midday, Jennifer was relieved A screeching tyre of a post van as it parked outside 25 Queen Street. Jennifer stood still, hoping the stranger was knocking on someone else's door. The van door slammed violently, and light footsteps were becoming louder approaching her door.

Knock, Knock.

Jennifer was walking slowly to the door and stared at the intruder through the peephole.

The postman noticed a hole in the lower part of the wooden front door and glimpsed an elderly lady's slipper. He rang the doorbell twice and knocked on the door with his knuckles.

"Damn, this postman is persistent. Go away. What am I going to do?"

"Madam, please open the door."

"Squawk, nobody is at home, come back later."

"Madam, please open the door. I have an important letter which needs to be delivered and signed for today."

"I'm not a madam. I'm a parrot, squawk, come back later. Nobody is at home, come back later, squawk."

Endurance boot camp

In a secret military base in USA, Colonel A. R. Sole was teaching the new recruits the pain endurance.

"My name is Colonel A. R. Sole. Today you will learn how to endure pain. Because a real soldier does not feel any pain during military training exercising, or when on a secret mission. Men who show pain are whingers and weak."

"Do you feel pain?"

"No, sir"

"Great. Remove all your shoes and socks!"

Colonel A. R Sole stamped and walked on a soldier's feet.

"Did you feel any pain, soldier?"

"No, sir, because I am a soldier."

"Great answer."

In the row of soldiers, there was 5 feet and 2 inches tall man with a skinny physique; the bones were so easy to be counted. Colonel A. R Sole noticed him and approached him.

"What is your name, soldier?"

"My name is Nicholas Whiningnomore, sir," saluting him.

 "Do you believe you are strong enough for any pain endurance?"

"Yes, sir; don't be fool by my undersized stature and rudimentary muscles - I am strong as the other giant and brawny soldiers."

The other soldiers burst out laughing.

"I like your confidence. Let's put it to the test!"

Colonel A. R. Sole stamped and walked up and down presumably on the skinny soldier's feet.

"Did you feel any pain, Nicholas Whiningnomore?"

"No, sir."

"Because you are a soldier."

"No, sir. Because they were not my feet. They were his" pointing at a soldier to his left, who placed his right hand in his mouth attempting to block screams of agony.

The Deacons' final test

In a spare room of the church Saint Peter, Bishop Luke supervises the final test for the deacons. A bell has been placed on each deacon's private parts, and it will chime if the deacon has been emotionally compromised; only those deacons who can control his emotions pass this final test.

"Today, this is your final challenge; be strong and keep control your emotions. You will pass this final test."

"Thank you, Bishop Luke."

Michelle enters the room.

"Michelle, how many times do I need to tell you? It is not appropriate wearing a miniskirt in a church. I can clearly see your G-string thong, and your top is too tight - your breast is almost popping out."

"I'm sorry Bishop Luke. I was getting changed when the phone rang. The archbishop is coming to see you in 30 minutes."

"Thank you, Michelle."

Ding! Ding! Ding!

"Peter, you have failed the final test. Don't worry, you'll be able to re-sit it next year."

Five minutes later, Michelle renters the room wearing a white towel after she has had a shower. Her dog Jesse follows her.

"Jesse! Don't pull my towel! Behave, Jesse!"

Jesse starts barking and pulls the towel down.

"No, Jesse, bad dog. I'm so embarrassed."

Michelle reacts and covers her lady parts with her arms and hands."

The deacons remain unmoved by the embarrassing scenery.

"Here I come. I come to the rescue, Michelle."

Sebastian, Michelle's gay best friend, enters the room trotting, holding a dress.

"Hello handsome!"

"He is hot! Look at his biceps."

"I like his peachy bottom. I want to touch it."

"I'm wondering if he is free tonight."

Some deacons are thinking.

"Michelle, you embarrass me again!"

"I'm sorry Bishop Luke I was having a shower when someone knocked on the door. The archbishop is here."

"Okay get dressed; we don't want the archbishop to see what is going on!"

"That is why Sebastian is here. I am ready for going out. I put my mascara on, my red lipstick and my party clothes. "

"Let's go, Michelle."

"Let's go, Sebastian."

Sebastian and Michelle trot out of the room.

Ding! Ding! Ding! Ding!

"Wait for us!" the deacons exclaim.

Ding! Ding! Ding! Ding!

"Do not leave me behind," Bishop Luke adds.

Edward Brown

Edward Brown was born and lived most of his life in York. He felt he was at home in York; he found people were friendly, caring, and full of life. During the day he was working in an office in a financial company, and in his spare time, he was a volunteer in some of the charity shops. He wanted to give back to the community for the less fortunate. The community loved him. He was always generous towards other people. He loved all the seasons, apart from winter. He did not enjoy walking on the pavements when it was cold or frosty. He was scared, he might fall and break some of his bones. He was always careful walking on frosty or iced pavements. The years went by quickly and one day, in his sixties, he was going to the supermarket, and he did not notice there was a black ice on the pavement. He slipped and fell badly, breaking his knees and wrists. After several months, his bones healed from the bad fall. Every time the weather was turning cold, a freezing shiver went down his spine. It was like if the bones knew already the winter was coming.

His best friend John suggested to spend the winter months in Turkey. Turkey was much warmer all the year around comparing with the UK and the weather in winter was milder, so no frost or black ice were in sight. Edward enjoyed so much he decided to move permanently. He continued to be generous to his neighbours, and the community welcomed him like an uncle or half-brother. He spent all the remaining years in Turkey and, when he passed away, the community mourned his death for seven days. God was so moved he welcomed him to Heaven.

Edward never complained in his life; however, he was completely sad in Heaven and Saint Peter heard about his grievance, he wanted to make Edward happy again.

"Hi Edward; how are you enjoying Heaven?"

"Hi Saint Peter, I love to be in Heaven. I am so grateful to hear God, listen to the angels' hymns and to hear the angels playing the harps, but I know it is odd. I should not feel this way, because I do not have a body anymore. I am only a spirit. I feel freezing."

"That is odd."

"Would it be possible to place me somewhere else there is not a breeze coming through?"

"There is not a place in Heaven which is warmer. There is a place outside Heaven where you will feel much warmer. However, I need to ask God if he allows me to send you there."

"Yes, Saint Peter; please ask God if he allows it."

God was reluctant for him to be relocated in Purgatory but, after being convinced by Saint Peter, He agreed.

A week later, Saint Peter visited Edward Brown in Purgatory.

"Hi Edward; I hope you are much happier in Purgatory, and, with time, you'll adjust to the afterlife and move back to Heaven."

"Hi, Saint Peter; Purgatory is a better place for me. There are days when new souls had been sent here and I can feel freezing draughts, so I am wondering if you have any other places I can stay, I will be so eternally grateful."

"Your request brings me sadness. I am going to talk to God. If he can fulfil your needs, I am sure he will do everything in his power."

God heard Saint Peter's pleadings, with sadness in his heart, he allowed Edward Brown to be relocated to Hell. The devil was so overjoyed, he threw a party for Edward Brown. Every demon was wearing a party hat and some pulled party poppers. The party was in full swing; the devil, all the demons and other tormented souls were dancing the conga. The devil was wearing a party hat and blowing a foil blowout. In his eyes full of fire, he saw another soul to be tormented for eternity, and Edward Brown finally found a place where he would never feel cold again.

One day Saint Peter visited Hell and, as soon as he opened the door, a voice yelled:

"Close that blood door, brr; it is freezing outside!"

The three-way race

Screeching, bang, bang! The Fiat 500's engine sputtered, and the car stopped on a hard shoulder of M1 motorway.

A red Porsche 911 Carrera was following behind.

The Porsche driver stepped out of the car and offered assistant to the stranding motorist.

"Are you okay? Do you need any assistance?"

"My old Fiat 500 had broken down. Can you help me?"

"Of course. I will tow your car with mine. Please turn on your indicator when we are in proximity to the next garage."

"I will; thank you for your help."

The red Porsche was towing along the stranded Fiat 500. A Ferrari 512 BB overtook the Porsche, and the driver was revving his powerful engine; it was his way of showing off that his car was better than anyone else's.

The Porsche's driver felt insulted. He chased the Ferrari and overtook it. He smirked at him. He hated bullies.

The Ferrari driver could not stand being second, so he chased the Porsche driver and repassed him. The Ferrari and Porsche started to race for 3 miles, until the Porsche driver noticed a sign of a garage in the next half a mile.

A police car was parked on the hard shoulder, the policeman was holding a digital tachometer laser speed-gun. He was flabbergasted to see a Ferrari 512 BB and a red Porsche 911 Carrera racing each other, and an old Fiat 500 was trying to overtake both!

Can I clean your car, Sir?

John had few visitors knocking on his door. He had lived in his house for the last fifteen years. He never complained about it. When people were knocking on his door, he felt someone cared about him. One day he was watching a football match on TV in his bedroom when he heard "knock, knock."

"I wonder who could be? Maybe a Jehovah Witness trying to persuade me to listen to the Bible and God. I am not a very religious person. They are wasting their time. Could it be a salesperson? That is most probable. I would not buy anything face-to-face, or over the phone. I buy products or services only if I know, like and trust the person. I have been brought up this way. There are so many people in the world who are doing anything to scam you."

He walked down the stairs, hoping the annoying caller would have already left, instead of waiting for someone to open the front door.

He turned the key and sighed to get strength for talking to a stranger. He opened the door, and he was dumfounded. Five children, from 10 to 15 years old, were standing in front of his door holding a bucket full of water and washing-up liquid and a rectangular, yellow sponge.

"Good afternoon, sir. Our family is struggling financially -we have just enough money for the bare minimum. We thought we can go around to our neighbours to clean their cars."

"That is very thoughtful."

"My guess is you own this blue Ford Fiesta."

"Unfortunately, this car is not mine."

"I see"

"Peter, this gentleman is driving a better car than a Ford Fiesta. I reckon he drives this Audi Serie 3."

"Again, this is not my car. I like more sporty cars."

"Silly boys! My name is Jennifer. I am 15 years old. Look at his clothes and the watch he is wearing. Armani clothes and Rolex watch; I deduct this gentleman is wealthy. My guess is your car is this black Marcedes Benz."

"Unfortunately, you are all wrong."

"It is funny that, with all the doors in the street, you have knocked on my front door, but I don't own a car. I cycle everywhere, - I do not like polluting the environment."

The children walked away and knocked on the neighbouring door.

The Interview

John Smith is perfectionist in everything he does. He received an invitation to a job interview for an Assistant Accountant the following day, Tuesday, at 10:30 in the city centre of York. He searched for the company on Google, he prepared possible answers for the interview, and he had three questions for the interviewer.

His blue suit had already been dry-cleaned; his black shoes were polished. He felt he was ready mentally and prepared to overcome any challenge at the interview.

Tuesday morning, he got up at 8 o'clock. He shaved his beard and facial hair off and had a cold shower. The cold shower reinvigorated him. After a light breakfast, he got dressed. He checked his watch. It was 9 o'clock. He knew it was early. He did not want to turn up 20 minutes before the interview - if he showed up too early, he was too keen, and he would not get the job.

He was walking slowly to the bus stop, allowing time to pass by. He checked his watch; it was 9:30. At the bus stop, a pregnant woman was sitting on a bench. She appeared to be 9 months pregnant. 5 minutes passed and there was no sign of any bus in any direction. 10 minutes passed and John Smith was starting to be anxious. Few drops of sweat were rolling down his forehead. He had calculated the bus would have taken 30 minutes to reach the city centre. He needed 10 minutes to walk to the company where the interview was taking place. Fifteen minutes passed; again, there was no sign of the bus in any direction. John Smith started walking up and down on the pavement.

"Come on bus, I am waiting. Please turn up, I do not want to lose the opportunity of this exciting job."

He took courage and asked the lady sitting on the bench.

"I'm sorry, how long have you been waiting?"

"I have been waiting for 1 hour."

"Do you know when it is due?"

"It's due in 2 weeks." she rubbed her tummy.

"I can't wait for that long." His hand was shaking, he picked his phone up from the jacket and dialled a taxi. He was lucky, a taxi was just around the corner. He stepped inside and gave the address to the taxi driver. The taxi was driving fast on the road, trying to make up the lost time.

John Smith thought it was a good idea to call the company and explain that, due to circumstances out of his control, he was going to be late for the interview.

The receptionist informed him: "John Smith, I am checking your interview, and I can confirm your interview is tomorrow at 10:30."

A blood test

What a jovial atmosphere at 190 Melrosegate in York.

"Ha, ha!"

"Ha, ha!"

"I cannot believe the GP Surgery Medical Centre sent me a letter requesting me to take a blood test."

"That is funny, Paul."

"I know, Trevor. My guess is they have forgotten to update their database. Tomorrow, I will attend their appointment and have a word with their GP."

Next day, Paul left the house 2 hours before the blood test was due. He entered the GP Surgery Medical Centre in Tang Hall, York.

Paul approached the front desk.

"Are you okay, sir?"

"I'm fine, this is my natural colour."

"What a stench! Luke, are you still wearing that awful deodorant?"

"Yes Tracy. It's my favourite. It is called Lynx Africa, and all the women love it."

"I don't; I found it has a revolting smell."

"I am here for a blood test at 2 p.m."

"What is your name?"

"My name is Paul Robinson."

"Let's me check your details. I see you are early."

"I would like to speak to your available GP."

"The available GP is Roger Knowswell. Currently, he is on his lunch, and he does not have any appointment until 12:30. I'll talk to him, and I let you know when he is available. Please take a seat."

Five minutes passed.

"Mr Paul Robinson, Roger Knowswell can see you now. He is room 5."

Paul walked to room 5.

Knock, knock.

"Please come in."

Paul entered the room.

"What a stench!"

"I'm sorry it is my shirt. I have not had it cleaned for the last 2 weeks."

"It had not been cleaned for the last 2 years since I had been in a car accident."

"So how can I help you?"

"I have received this letter requesting me to take a blood test today."

"This is a general practice letter we send to all our patients for checking they are well and healthy. We have due care for our patients."

"I see. Would you be so kind as to check your database?"

"Of course; what is your name?"

"My name is Paul Robinson."

"I've found you. You were born on 17 May 1991, and you had never had any medical conditions. You are in perfect health."

"You are wrong. I died 2 years ago in a car accident."

"That is impossible. You are here talking to me. You cannot be a ghost; I'd see through you."

"I'm not a vampire, either; I will turn to ash as soon as I step out of my house."

"I have run out of ideas."

"I am a zombie."

Roger Knowswell's hands were shaking. In a moment of panic, he started dialling 911 from his desk telephone. The call was disconnected by Paul pulling out the telephone wire from the socket.

"Really? You are just calling the police. I will never eat your brain."

"You are a zombie."

"I'm a part of the Brain Elite Society. We don't just eat any brain. We are sophisticated and preselected. We eat only brains which are smart. Your brain is dumb. If I eat your brain, it will make me ill. Your first mistake was sending a letter requesting a blood test - it could have been avoided if you had updated your database. Your second mistake was not recognising I am a zombie by my stench smell and white colour of my skin. I will see you around, doc."

Training day

A business school had organised an event in its training room for businesswomen and businessmen, with the aim to help them to increase their revenue using computer tools and to acquire new customers with the latest techniques.

"Hello everyone, my name is Michelle White. I am your presenter for today. I will cover new computer tools for helping your businesses to increase your revenue, and new techniques to acquire new customers. I have a tight schedule, so please refrain from asking any questions. If you have any, please jot them down on a piece of paper. If I have not answered them during the day, I will reply to your questions during the q & a session. We will have 15-minute breaks during the morning and afternoon, and one hour for lunch."

"Hello, miss; my name is Peter Anderson. I have an important meeting at 16:30; do you believe we will finish the training before my meeting starts?"

"Yes, sir. My aims are finishing my training by 15:00 and cover all your questions in the q & a session no later than 16:00."

"Thank you."

The day was full of information and all the businesspeople felt overwhelmed with information. They refrained from asking any questions until the q & a.

"That concludes my training. Has anyone got any questions?"

Ten businesspeople raised their hands and Michelle White answered all their questions in full. It was 16:00.

"If anyone does have any more questions after today, you can reach us by email or phone; our contact details are on your training slides on your desk. You are now free to go and thank you for attending this training."

Peter Anderson checked his Rolex and placed all the paperwork and stationery in his briefcase. He rushed out to the nearest exit door.

"I'm sorry, sir. That is not the main exit."

Five minutes later, he entered the training room again and he was so humiliated his face turned red like ripe strawberry.

"I'm such a fool."

"Don't worry, sir, you are not the first, and won't be the last, person who has visited our walk-in storage room."

House party

In the canteen of a business company, the work colleagues were organising a house party.

"This weekend, it's your turn for the house party, Michael."

"No problem at all. I have already bought 6 bottles of beers, a bottle of tequila and whiskey, and some nibbles like: 4 tubes of *Pringles*, some *Walkers* crips and 4 pizzas. I have salt, but I run out of money, could anyone buy some lemons for the shots?"

"I'll do that, Michael."

"Thank you, Peter."

"What about the music?"

"I have bought the best party music. I am playing it in my hi-fi. I am even installed a revolving disco ball on my ceiling."

"That sounds awesome. I cannot wait."

"Me too. What time does the party start?"

"I was thinking about 10 p.m."

"That is fine."

On the day of the party, Michael was placing the crips in several bowls, waiting for the arrivals of his work colleagues. He was expecting 10 people to turn up. It was a mix of men and women. It was 10 p.m. Peter was the first to arrive, followed by John with his girlfriend, Michelle. Racheal invited her friend, Jennifer. Andrew came with

Tony, Jordan and Joseph from the IT department, followed by other people Michael did not recognise. The house was full of people, who were talking and dancing. There was so much noise, and Michael had to intervene many times to turn down the volume of the hi-fi.

"Tony, please stop turning up the volume. My neighbours will complain and call the police."

"Michael, I'm still hungry. Can you cook something?"

"Of course, Jordan. I will place the pizza in the oven. It will be ready in 15 minutes."

"Michael, it is tequila time. Tequila boom, boom. I have brought some lemons, let's have some shots."

"Okay, Peter."

"First, you place some salt on your hand and lick it; then you swallow a tequila shot and place a slice of lemon in your mouth."

"Tequila boom, boom."

The house party was in full swing. The guests were drinking tequila and beers and eating food. They were all wasted. They were enjoying themselves. It was 2 a.m.

"Guys and girls, it's 2 a.m. It is getting late."

"You are right, Peter."

"I think it is time to go home. Well done, Michael. This is the best party I have been to. I will never forget it."

"Michel, I have got some bad news. A police car had just parked in your driveway."

"You are kidding, Jordan."

"No, I am dead serious."

"Okay, I have a plan. Turn off all the lights and the hi-fi, and no one makes any sound. I got this."

Michael took off his clothes and put on his pyjamas.

Knock, knock.

"Open the door! This is the police!"

Michael switched on the landing lights and walked down the stairs.

He opened the front door and yawned.

A policeman and a policewoman were standing in front of his door, unimpressed.

"We have received a complaint from one of your neighbours of loud music and noises coming from this house. They believe you are having a party."

"Party? What party? I can guarantee there is no party in here. I have been sleeping in my bed all night. I see what is happening - one of my neighbours is a prankster. He loves calling the police and wasting their time!"

"We apologise for waking you up."

"Don't worry, officers."

Michael yawned, and closed the door.

The emergency

Nee-naw nee-naw nee-naw nee-naw.

The police car was driving fast on the road; all the cars, vans and buses let it through. The driver seemed to be possessed, like a F1 driver, and no one attempted in blocking its path.

Passers-by were gathering on the pavements, trying to guess the reason of this emergency. They had different points of view.

"I reckon the police car is chasing another vehicle."

"Where is the getaway car?"

"I don't think so. I presume the police car has been sent to assist in dealing with a bank robbery and possible hostages."

"Don't be daft! I believe this is a British incident of the Miami mall about the parallel portal and the giant grey Aliens."

The police car veered on to a left road. It drove for 2 miles and parked in a private driveway, screeching to a halt.

The policeman stepped out of the car and walked to a door.

Knock, knock.

"Hi, son, nice to see you."

"Dad, let me through."

The policeman walked up the stairs, taking two steps at the time. He barged into the bathroom. It was the silence before the storm.

"Pfft fraaap poot blat thppthtphphhph braaap braaaack frrrt blaaarp pbbbbt."

"When you've got to go, don't hold back."

The policeman came out of the bathroom and closed the door behind him.

"Dad, I just dropped a toxic bomb. If you care about your life, wait 30 minutes before you enter."

The 4 inseparable friends

Kiyoshi Hikari, Alberto Dileone, Frank Schneider, and John White were 4 inseparable friends, who shared the good and bad times together as a group for over 20 years. They met in holiday in Rome, Italy in 2001, and they always kept in touch.

Twenty-two years later, John White organised for them all to meet each other in an English pub in York.

"We have been best friends for over 20 years. We are all now 50 years old. I was thinking of jumping out of a plane and deploying a parachute. I am in."

"John, is it safe?"

"Yes, Kiyoshi, the chances of the main and reserve parachutes both malfunctioning are very slim."

"Before we jump out of the plane, the organiser will check all our parachutes. The yellow lever deploys the main parachute. The black lever deploys the reserve parachute."

"I am not afraid. My surname, Dileone, means 'lion'. Lions are fearless. I am in."

"If Alberto is in, I am too. My grandfather was a fearless Japanese pilot in World War 2."

"Awesome! What about you, Frank Schneider? Are you in?"

"If you buy me a chocolate bar, two German sausages and a pint of beer, I am in."

"Done! We will meet tomorrow at noon, at the private hangar outside Leeds. I will text all of you the address."

Next day, the inseparable friends met at the private hangar. Ther organiser checked all the parachutes and gave the final instructions.

The plane took off and reached 10,000 feet.

The pilot confirmed the altitude and opened the hatch.

"Who is the first person to dare jumping out?"

"That will be me, John!", Kiyoshi exclaimed.

Kiyoshi jumped out of the plane. He enjoyed doing stunts in the air. His body was plunging down fast. He deployed the main parachute. It malfunctioned. He attempted to deploy the reserve parachute. It malfunctioned as well.

His final word was "kamikaze!" before dying on the ground.

"I will be next," John added, before jumping out of the plane.

A breeze went through his short, grey hair. At 5000 feet altitude he deployed his main parachute.

While he was descending, his words were "God, save the King!"

Ten minutes later he gracefully touched down.

In the meantime, Frank Schneider was eating a chocolate bar and 2 German sausages, washed down with a pint of German beer. He was wearing the biggest parachute, due to his enormous belly and bottom.

"I am ready."

He jumped out of the plane. His body was plunging down very fast. He deployed the main parachute. The fibres of the suspension lines holding the main parachute started to fray and the cloth canopy blew away. In a moment of panic, Frank deployed the reserve parachute. Again, the fibres of the suspension lines holding the reserve parachute started to fray and the cloth canopy blew away.

His final words were "Königsberg klopse" (translation meatballs) before making a big hole and dying in the ground.

The pilot noticed the organiser forgot to supply Alberto Dileone with a parachute.

Alberto was fine. He opened a vacuum flask. He poured two servings of coffee into a plastic mug and drank it. He jumped out of the plane without a parachute.

His body was plunging down at an incredible speed. He came back up. He plunged down again. He came back up again.

Ten minutes later he touched the ground.

John approached him and he was curious to find how he had survived without a parachute.

"Before I jumped out of the plane, I drank Lavazza coffee. The more you go down, the more it pulls you up."

My girlfriend is from up North

Paul Robinson had arranged a meet up with his best friend, James, and his girlfriend, Jennifer, in a local pub after 5 p.m. Paul was so excited he had finally found his soulmate, and her name was Clara Richmond.

James was drinking a pint of *Irn-Bru* and Jennifer was snacking cheese & onion Walkers crisps in a private room upstairs in the pub.

Paul walked into the room, shielding Clara's entrance. They sat in the stalls.

James stopped drinking and Jennifer paused snacking. They seemed to be frozen.

"Thank you both for coming today. This is my new girlfriend, Clara Richmond. For the last 10 years, I have been in speed-dating in my local pub. Even though I liked some women I met, and I wanted to see them again after the first date, they did not feel the same way. One day, I met Clara and we both felt the same way. We finished each other's sentences. We both laughed at the same jokes. The more time we spent together, the more we wanted to see each other. Finally, I had found my soulmate. After 3 months, Clara confessed she had a secret she needed to tell me. It could change our relationship. I said that as long as she was not a man, nothing would change my feelings for her. She replied she concealed her identity, because some people would faint, or behave aggressively towards her, if she were to reveal herself. She transformed in front of my eyes as she is now. I said that at least she was not a man! She was fine as she was. She burst out laughing."

James and Jennifer were listening very carefully. James had always been a very talkative person, but in this instance he was quiet.

"Are you okay, James?

"I'm thinking."

"So, where was I? Her name is Clara, but her true name is difficult to pronounce, and the last three vowels are so high-pitched that they can break a glass. Clara prefers to use the English first name. Not many people know her identity and the select few are the luckiest ones. Slowly, the community is embracing Clara as a long-distant auntie."

"Jennifer and I are so lucky."

"Yes, you are."

"Look at the time! It's time for ladies' room."

"Can I join you, Jennifer?"

"Hey, Clara, the more the merrier."

Jennifer and Clara left the room.

"Wow, I did not expect that. Did you notice Clara is different from us?"

"What are you talking about?"

"I have noticed that Clara has 4 arms and 4 hands."

"That is very handy. I wish I had 4 arms and 4 hands. You know that I deliver newspapers almost every day. It is fine when the weather is nice, but not when it rains. Have you tried to hold an umbrella and, with the other hand, lift the letterbox and push through the newspaper inside the house? It is mission impossible. I am so glad I bought a waterproof jacket and trousers, so I have both hands free."

"I can imagine. What about her hair?"

"What is wrong with her hair?"

"Her hair is green!"

"Your hair is blonde. Mine is black. Jennifer is dark blonde. I have seen people who had blue or pink hair. One time, my granny went to the hair salon and her hairstylist dyed her hair. When she came back home, my mum and I noticed her hair was brown, with a green reflection in the mirror. My granny was enraged, like the Incredible Hulk and told off the hairstylist over the phone. She told him to fix her hair the next day."

"Okay, Paul what about the three eyes? What are you going to say about it?"

"The two eyes are like ours. The third eye is special, because she can look deep inside you and see if you are telling the truth, or you are lying. She will be very useful for our criminal justice."

"She is different from us."

"Of course, she is. You are different from me. Jennifer is different from you. Everyone is different. Clara is different. What are you saying James?"

"She is an alien."

"Omg, I did not see that coming! You are racist."

"I am not racist."

"Clara is coming from Proxima b, 4.22 light years away. I don't mind she is an Alien because I love her, and she loves me back. She is the most important person in my life."

Jennifer and Clara re-entered the room.

"What did you talk about in my absence?"

"We talked about your differences from us, Clara."

"Have you talked about the big news to James?"

"I didn't have a chance. James was so obsessed with your differences that I did not mention the big news."

"I'm pregnant and we have triplets on the way."

"There will be three more of your kind?"

James fainted. His head was resting on the pine table.

"I don't understand why he fainted. He is not the father."

"I know Paul. When I told you I was pregnant, you were jumping around the room, and you were so overjoyed."

"I was happy just to have a child. I will have three, and a girlfriend to love and share my life with."

Not the getaway car

Knock, knock.

Sandy was delighted. She knew who was knocking on the door.

"Finally, after a week, Paul is back. I was so worried and sick something terrible had happened to him. I am very upset with him. He never called. He didn't text. I am going to tell him off, but first, I want to kiss him and hug him. I missed him so much."

Sandy rushed down the stairs and opened the front door. Her happiness turned to sadness. Her eyes were full of tears. Two police officers were standing there, with a gloomy expression.

"Is your name Sandy Thorpe?"

"Yes."

"My name is Constable George Smith and this my colleague, Mat Ings. Can we come in? We have got something to tell you."

"Of course, officers, please come in."

It seemed that 30 years had passed. Sandy felt she aged like an elderly lady and every step on the stairs was a daunting task. She placed her hand on the handrail to facilitate her movement. Her breathing was heavy and difficult. She was relieved when she saw the landing in front of her eyes.

They walked into the living room.

"Can you make some tea with milk and sugar? It had been a tough day. It has been cold. We have walked all day. We didn't stop talking to the public."

"Certainly, officers. Can I serve you some chocolate digestive with the tea?"

"That is my favourite biscuit."

In the kitchen, Sandy picked three mugs, and one of them was her gift to Paul with an inscription of her deepest affection on the porcelain - "I will always love you." Tears rolled down her cheeks and a flash memory popped into her head. Every time Sandy made a cup of tea she picked this mug, and Paul's face lit up with joy.

"I would never make any more cups of tea for Paul and see his face light up. I miss you, Paul."

Blub, blurp, blup, blup; the kettle was boiling the water. Sandy poured the hot water into the mugs after pouring the milk and dropping in a teabag and some sugar. She placed the mugs on a tray, together with a plate of chocolate digestive biscuits.

"Where was I? Oh yes, a week ago Paul Robinson went to a business meeting. His intention was to drive there, but his car broke down. He called the mechanic, who informed him he did not know what was wrong with his car. The mechanic put Paul's car in the recovery vehicle and drove to his garage. It would take him at least several days to discover the fault. Paul Robinson decided to travel by train. It was a more relaxing and safer journey. Later that day, the twin brothers Brown heisted over £10 million from the Royal Bank of Scotland. The police had chased their car, until they crashed into a house. The twin brothers escaped. They were armed and dangerous, and we informed the public not to approach them. Last night, they had been spotted near the garage where Paul Robison's Ford Fiesta had been parked. They thought that Ford cars were reliable, and it would be a good idea to steal this car. Andrew, the oldest brother by 2 minutes, used a wrecking bar and opened the door, unaware of a man who was walking with his dog, and who noticed the crime and phoned 999. My colleague and I were in the area. We called for back-up and approached the vehicle by crawling on the ground. The twin brothers were unaware that the Ford Fiesta in question was broken down. They pulled out the cables of the immobilizer. When all their efforts failed miserably, they stepped out the car and we arrested them."

"I'm sorry to interrupt you, George, that was not what happened. We were about to arrest them when they kicked us in our privates."

"We started to sing *Staying Alive* by the Bee Gees. We gave them a Glasgow kiss."

"You are an English person, so you might not know what a Glasgow kiss is. It is a sharp, sudden headbutt to their nose. They will be in pain for several days. We handcuffed them and the streets are safer now. We also retrieved the 10 million. The Ford Fiesta was not the getaway car."

"I thought you came to tell my boyfriend; Paul, had died."

"We do not know anything about Paul Robinson. We just came to report the twin brothers attempt to steal his car."

The police officers drank the tea and had some chocolate digestive biscuits.

Next day, Paul Robinson turned up. Sandy was relieved, and told him off. Paul explained he was staying in a four-stars hotel in another city, where it had been flooded. All the telephone lines had been disconnected, so he could not call or text. He made up with Sandy with a romantic dinner in an expensive restaurant. Before the dinner, he called the mechanic, who informed him that there was not point in fixing the car due to the twin brothers pulling out the immobilizer cables. The cost of the repair will be extortionate, and he will be better off buying a new car. Paul informed the car insurance company, and they advised him to scrap the car; due to the increase in the car premium, he would only receive Ł3 credited to his bank account. He was devasted. He loved his Ford Fiesta. It was his first car and, five years ago, he paid Ł600 to a private seller.

A bank heist

"After 3 months of reversal, today is the day we become filthy rich."

"Yes boss."

"I cannot wait to count the money!"

"Yes, we need to follow our first rule. We are no longer call each other by our names. If we do, the police will identify us. Each of us has an animal name. I'm the eagle, because I supervise the entire operation. You are called Tom and Jerry; you are always pranking each other. You are called giraffe because you are tall. You are called skunk; I do not need to explain why."

"Eagle, may I have a different animal name?"

"I'm sorry, animal names had been picked. At 10:50 we enter the bank. At 11.00 we rob the bank. Let's check if we are ready. Everyone is wearing dark clothes, including gloves. A gun should be placed in your back trousers pocket. Wrap your shoes in plastic bags so you don't leave any footprints. The last item is a mask. Did everyone buy a Micky Mouse mask?"

"Eagle, I have tried to buy a Micky Mouse mask for six months, however they are sold out. My only options were Minnie or Pluto."

"Giraffe, you don't have the body or voice for impersonating her."

"Ha, ha, you are so hilarious, Tom."

"Do not worry, I bought Pluto instead."

"Great! Four Micky Mouse and 1 Pluto, a mismatch of bank robbers."

"Let's synchronise our watches."

"Let's go animals!"

They entered the bank as planned. There were a few customers waiting in a queue at the counter. They looked at their watch - it was 10.57.

"Pfft, fraaap, poot."

"I'm sorry, Eagle, I have done a big one."

"Skunk, you should have held on."

"I cannot smell anything, Skunk."

"Don't attract attention. Act casual."

A woman was standing in the queue reading a newspaper when the intense odour overpowered her, and she fainted.

"It's time animals; let's wear our masks."

Eagle drew the gun from of his back trouser pocket.

"Everyone, this is a bank robbery. Lie down on the ground. I do not want to shoot anyone; don't be a hero today. Including you, security guy, slowly pick up your gun, place it down on the floor and kick it towards me."

"Good, it will be soon over, and you go on with your day."

Eagle approached the bank counter and talked to the young bank clerk. She had blue eyes and blonde hair.

"You don't need to lie down, please stand up! Open the bank safe and place all the money into these travel bags."

The young bank clerk coughed.

"Hurry up!"

She coughed again.

"You should see a doctor; your cough sounds nasty."

She pointed a piece of paper Sellotaped on the glass bank counter.

"Sorry for the inconvenience, yesterday the Beagle bank robbers stole all the money and gold in the bank safe. We are asking our customers to start again depositing so we can continue lending and offering savings. Thank you for your understanding."

"I cannot believe it. Do I understand your safe is empty and are you asking customers to deposit money?"

She nodded.

"I can't; my last money was spent on this gun."

"Do you have any money, Giraffe?"

"I'm sorry, Eagle, I spent my remaining money on a Pluto mask."

"What about you, Tom and Jerry?"

"This morning, we paid for everyone's breakfast and we are skint."

"What about you, Skunk?"

"I paid for everyone's bus tickets and I'm skint, too. Oops, I have done it again. It's Tom and Jerry's fault. They shouldn't buy baked beans!"

"Eagle, have we all done this for nothing?"

"Apparently, Giraffe, it had been a waste of time!"

They walked out of the bank empty-handed.

The demolition man

"Tonight, we are going to bed early. I do not want a repeat of being late. This morning, you were late at school, and I was late for work."

"Mum, tonight my football team is playing, and I will miss the match."

"I understand, Daniel; if you watch it, we end up going to bed late again. Don't worry, I'll record it and you watch it tomorrow after school."

"I'm not happy."

"I'll make it up to you. Go to sleep and do not let the bugs bite."

Next day, it was 7 am. Beep, beep, beep, Mollie turned off the alarm clock.

"It's time to get up, sleepyheads!"

She entered the children's bedroom, and they were still sleeping.

"Hurry up, don't force me to pull the duvet off."

They didn't move.

"You have been warned."

Mollie pulled off the duvet and Daniel and Gemma jumped out of the bed. The children went to the bathroom and, after brushing their teeth and washing their faces, they walked down the stairs and entered the living room. Mollie had prepared breakfast, with jam &

toast, bowls of milk and cornflakes, and glasses of orange juice.

They had breakfast and Mollie helped Gemma and Daniel to get ready for school. They stepped into the car. It was 8 o'clock. She drove to their school and then to her job.

It was 8:10 when three suspicious-looking men were standing outside 91 Queen Street.

"This is the house we need to knock down."

"Are you sure, Stuart?"

"Yes, I am. I have the paperwork and the authorisation."

"We don't have enough manpower."

"Jack don't be silly. More manpower is on its way in a couples of hours, and a wrecking-ball will help us to knock down this house."

"Okay, Stuart"

Stuart used a wrecking-bar to open the door.

"First, Jack, check all the rooms to make sure no one is in the house. Robert, turn off the gas supply."

Ten minutes later, Jack reported to Stuart.

"No one is in."

"Great! Jack, now turn off the water."

"Yes, Stuart."

"Stuart, are you 100% positive this is the house we need to knock down? Because I found the house is well-decorated and looks lived in by a family."

"Yes Jack, it is. These squatters do anything to pretend they have rights to live in this house."

They began to knock down walls and demolished anything in their paths. Several hours later a wrecking-ball arrived, and more manpower joined the demolition team.

A gathering of people was shooting videos and texting and watching the house 91 Queen Street been torn apart.

Meanwhile, the other side of town, Mollie had arrived at work.

"I'm sorry, Trevor, for being late yesterday. My children kept me watching tv and the following day it was difficult to wake them up."

"Don't worry, Mollie, I have children too. Since I have a routine in place, they never go to bed late, and they always wake up with energy and feel refreshed."

Mollie had kept her phone on silent. Her phone was vibrating all day by the missed phone calls and the unanswered messages.

"Mollie, your phone has been vibrating all day."

"I know, Janet, most of the times I receive many phone calls from salespeople and, no matter what I tell them, they keep phoning me. I am now ignoring them."

Mollie had been busy working all day by speaking to customers and solving queries. She was exhausted. She was looking forward to coming back home, relaxing and watching tv.

She picked her children up from school.

"How was your day?"

"It was good, mum; I have learned so much."

"I have enjoyed playing football with my classmates."

"Great; I had a busy day, so I decided to order some pizza and some ice cream."

"You are the best mum."

They were stuck in a traffic jam. Mollie checked her phone. 30 new messages came through. She dialled her voicemail.

"You have 30 new messages. Press 1 to listen to your first message."

"Forget it!"

She was relieved to see her street.

"Mum, where is the house?"

"What do you mean, Daniel? The house is there!"

Mollie stepped out of the car, and she was shocked. Her Victorian house, on which she had spent 20 years paying the mortgage and made many sacrifices due the loss of her husband from cancer, was rubble. The front door was the only spart standing up intact.

"Omg, my beautiful house. Who has demolished my house?"

"Calm down, lady!" Stuart shouted.

Mollie looked at Stuart. He was wearing an orange T-shirt, which was too small, showing off a heat burn on his stomach, and shorts. Due to his round belly and large bottom, he looked like a jammed strawberry doughnut which had a head, legs, and arms.

"Have you demolished my house?"

"Yes, I have, and these are the rulings."

Mollie checked the official documents.

"You have knocked down the wrong house. The number had been flipped."

Stuart realized that 19 Queen Street should have been knocked down, and his face turned red.

"I'm terribly sorry."

White smoke was exiting from Mollie's nose and ears. Her foot was moving backward and forward like a bull ready for charging.

"Run away, run away!" Mollie shouted.

Stuart and the other workers jumped in the van and the van sped away.

Gemma pulled Mollie's skirt.

"What are we going to do, mum?"

"The house needs more wood, bricks, paint. We will be okay, Gemma."

As soon as she replied, the front door collapsed.

"Where are we going to live, mum?"

"Don't worry, Daniel, we will stay with your grandad for a while."

"No grandad, please; every day he talks about War World 2. He is like a broken record." "Life is not fair!" Daniel exclaimed.

"Tell me about it; but at least we've still got each other."

Other Publications: Entertainment

Tickle Heart Vol.2
This is a collection of English funny short stories.

Thrumming Heart.
This a spellbinding English collection of fantasy, sci-fi, detective and paranormal short stories. It received a bronze medal in the Global Book Awards in 2021 and it became an Amazon best-seller in December 2022. The book is available in e-book, paperback and audio book formats. It will be available as graphic novel in the future.

Timothy Divine and His Adventures.
This is my first English novel, and tells the story of Timothy Divine, 10-year-old boy exploring new worlds in his rocket ship and interacting with his grandfather, Joe, and his friends. The novel has a lot of funny and emotional moments, which I am sure the reader will enjoy and share with family and friends.

Dr Victor Slater and The World.
This is my second English novel, in which the author tells how Dr Victor Slater and humanoid dinosaurs worked together in protecting Eart from the invasion of an evil alien race, Y42. In this novel, the reader will come across a love triangle, comedy and drama.

Printed in Great Britain
by Amazon